WELCOME TO THE 2020 CHELSEA ANNUAL!

We have packed into these pages all the information you could ever want about Chelsea and our players, including everything you need to know about this season's new arrivals, American winger Christian Pulisic, and new head coach and Chelsea legend Frank Lampard.

You can get to know the team better, as members of this year's squad talk about their early careers and reveal the moments that made them the world-class players they are today.

Plus, we look back at last season and our moment of glory in the Europa League final in detail, as well as celebrating two big anniversaries; 50 years after Chelsea's first-ever FA Cup victory and a decade since our only domestic Double so far.

There are also plenty of puzzles and quizzes for you to test your skill and show off your knowledge of the Blues, and even the chance to win a shirt signed by the team in our fantastic competition.

We hope you love it.

Happy reading!

Stamford and Bridget

NET!

Chelsea lifted European silverware again in 2019 as a 4-1 win over Arsenal in Azerbaijan gave us our second Europa League victory in six years, and the sixth continental trophy in our history.

2018/19 SEASON REVIEW

For the third year in a row, Chelsea ended the season with silverware in our hands, and this time it was the Europa League trophy, but the Blues also secured our place back in the Champions League with a third-place finish in the Premier League. Let's see how it all played out...

Chelsea's 2018/19 season began impressively as we won our first six matches at the start of an incredible 19-game unbeaten run across all competitions at the start of what turned out to be Maurizio Sarri's only season in charge. The highlights were a late Marcos Alonso clincher in a dramatic 3-2 home win over Arsenal and Ross Barkley's injury-time equaliser in a 2-2 draw with Manchester United.

In the meantime, we sailed through our Europa League group, winning five and drawing one of our six matches to qualify in top spot. Along the way, Ruben Loftus-Cheek bagged his first-ever hat-trick as we beat BATE Borisov at Stamford Bridge and Callum Hudson-Odoi scored his first senior goal in the home win over PAOK Salonika.

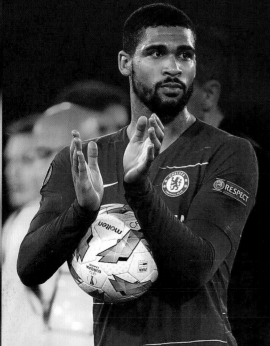

The Blues also embarked on a Carabao Cup run in the early stages of the season, which began with a great 2-1 win against Liverpool at Anfield. Emerson Palmieri got his first Chelsea goal and then Eden Hazard sent us through with one of his best goals with an incredible solo run and finish. We then progressed past Frank Lampard's Derby County with a close-run 4-2 win, before defeating Bournemouth in the quarter-finals.

The Carabao Cup semi-final was a two-legged tie against Tottenham and it proved to be a classic. Although we played well at Wembley, we lost 1-0 in the away leg but we turned it round in the second game with a 2-1 win at the Bridge, which took it to a penalty shootout! All four Chelsea players scored their kicks, but Spurs couldn't match us and Kepa saved Lucas Moura's effort to see us into the final!

The final also went to penalties, but it ultimately ended in disappointment against Manchester City at Wembley, despite Chelsea having created the better chances to win the Cup. This was a more promising display against the eventual Premier League champions after we had lost 6-0 to them in the league two weeks previously. It was time for us to bounce back.

Although it was clear the Premier League title race was between Man City and Liverpool, the race for the other two Champions League spots was on and we responded immediately to the Carabao Cup final loss with two vital wins, against Tottenham and Fulham, where Jorginho's belter helped to set us up for a late charge.

Meanwhile, the Europa League knockout rounds were underway and Chelsea cruised past Malmo, Dynamo Kiev and Slavia Prague to reach the semi-finals, winning the home and away legs of all three ties. Olivier Giroud was in fine goal-scoring form in Europe, while Willian led the way for assists in the competition.

The semi-final pitted us against in-form German side Eintracht Frankfurt and it was a dramatic tie indeed. We went a goal behind in the away leg, but Pedro's equaliser made us favourites at the halfway stage. However, the second leg also ended 1-1, so we had another penalty shootout at the Bridge! This time, Kepa was the hero as he stopped two Frankfurt spot kicks to ensure victory.

A tense last few weeks in the Premier League ended with us clinching third place in the league, with the highlight being another piece of individual wizardry from Hazard to set up a 2-0 win against West Ham at Stamford Bridge in April. Then, after beating Watford 3-0 in early May, it was official – Chelsea were back in the Champions League!

The season came to an end with the Europa League final in Baku and, for the first time in history, a European final was also a London derby, as we took on Arsenal. Naturally, the Blues came out on top, dominating the second half as we finished the season on a high with a convincing 4-1 victory. Giroud got the first and finished as the Europa League's top scorer with 11, Pedro added a second, then Hazard bagged a brace in what turned out to be his final game for the club. London was blue and Chelsea had won our sixth European trophy.

UEFA EUROPA LEAGUE 11

BAKU FINAL 2019

RETURN OF A LEGEND

In June, Chelsea announced our new head coach would be none other than Chelsea hero, Frank Lampard, much to the joy of Blues fans everywhere.

LOVING THE CHALLENGE

Lampard was unveiled to the media just before we went away for our pre-season preparations and described the job as the "greatest challenge" so far in his career. It was clear from the start he couldn't wait to get going.

For the supporters who were so used to watching him in the blue of Chelsea, seeing him in a suit on the sidelines has taken some getting used to, but he is every inch the modern coach. At the age of 41, he is a young boss, but he has the respect of everyone in football for what he achieved as a player and for the way he began his coaching career at Derby County.

With his former Chelsea team-mate Petr Cech returning to the club as a technical and performance advisor, there's a familiar feel to the setup this season! As Frank said when he started his new job, "The opportunity to come and manage this club, these fans, these players, was huge."

SHOW US YOUR MEDALS!

In his 13 years as a Chelsea player, between 2001 and 2014, Lampard established himself as one of our greatest ever. He played 648 games for the Blues, placing him fourth in our all-time appearances list, and scored 211 goals, which makes him Chelsea's top goalscorer of all time. Between 2005 and 2010, he scored at least 20 goals in every season...from midfield, no less. No wonder the fans call him 'Super Frank'!

In that time, Lampard also won 11 major trophies and managed to collect all the big domestic and European medals at club level. Let's break that down just so we can take in his legendary credentials: three Premier League titles, four FA Cups, two League Cups, the Champions League and the Europa League. As a three-time winner of the Chelsea Player of the Year award, there really is nothing Lampard didn't achieve here as a player.

FRANKS FOR THE MEMORIES

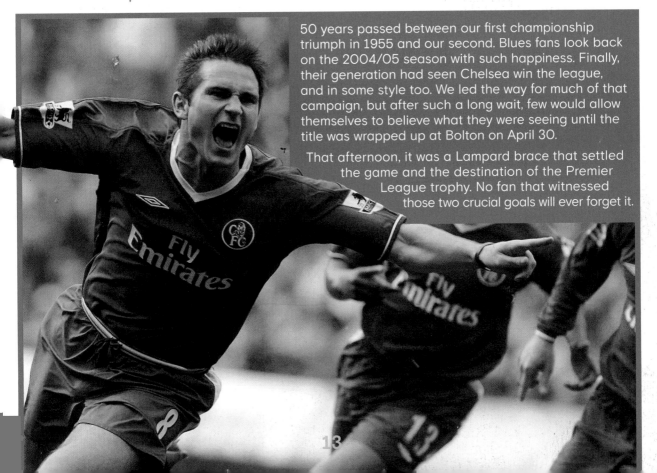

50 years passed between our first championship triumph in 1955 and our second. Blues fans look back on the 2004/05 season with such happiness. Finally, their generation had seen Chelsea win the league, and in some style too. We led the way for much of that campaign, but after such a long wait, few would allow themselves to believe what they were seeing until the title was wrapped up at Bolton on April 30.

That afternoon, it was a Lampard brace that settled the game and the destination of the Premier League trophy. No fan that witnessed those two crucial goals will ever forget it.

KEPA ARRIZABALAGA

Position: Goalkeeper
Date of birth: 03.10.94
Nationality: Spanish
Signed from: Athletic Bilbao
CFC apps: 54

Did You Know? Kepa is the 13th Spaniard to play for Chelsea in the Premier League era.

WILLY CABALLERO

Position: Goalkeeper
Date of birth: 28.09.81
Nationality: Argentinian
Signed from: Manchester City
CFC apps: 22

Did You Know? Willy won the Copa Libertadores – the South American equivalent of the Champions League – with Boca Juniors.

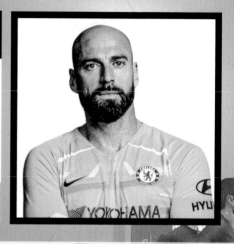

PLAYER PROFILES

MARCOS ALONSO

Position: Defender
Date of birth: 28.12.90
Nationality: Spanish
Signed from: Fiorentina
CFC apps: 120   CFC goals: 18

Did You Know? Marcos has scored the winning goal against both Tottenham Hotspur and Arsenal during his Chelsea career.

CESAR AZPILICUETA

Position: Defender
Date of birth: 28.08.89
Nationality: Spanish
Signed from: Marseille
CFC apps: 337   CFC goals: 9

Did You Know? Cesar is one of five players to captain Chelsea in a major European final, along with Ron Harris, Dennis Wise, John Terry and Frank Lampard.

ANDREAS CHRISTENSEN

Position: Defender
Date of birth: 10.04.96
Nationality: Danish
Source: Chelsea Academy
CFC apps: 72

Did You Know? Andreas was the only player to start all 15 of our Europa League matches on our way to lifting the trophy.

FIKAYO TOMORI

Position: Defender
Date of birth: 19.12.97
Nationality: English
Source: Chelsea Academy
CFC apps: 1

Did You Know? Fikayo was born in Calgary and even represented Canada at Under-20s level, but he has since won plenty of caps as part of England's Under-21 set up.

PLAYER PROFILES

EMERSON PALMIERI

Position: Defender
Date of birth: 03.08.94
Nationality: Italian
Signed from: Roma
CFC apps: 34   CFC goals: 1

Did You Know? Although he was born in Brazil, Emerson plays for Italy at international level after making his debut for the Azzurri in 2018.

ANTONIO RUDIGER

Position: Defender
Date of birth: 03.03.93
Nationality: German
Signed from: Roma
CFC apps: 89   CFC goals: 4

Did You Know? Antonio was named Man of the Match when we won the FA Cup at the end of his first season as a Blue in 2017/18.

All stats correct ahead of the 2019/20 season.

REECE JAMES

Position: Defender
Date of birth: 08.12.99
Nationality: English
Source: Chelsea Academy
CFC apps: 0

Did You Know? Reece was named Wigan's Player of the Year for 2018/19 after receiving an astonishing 96 per cent of the votes from Latics supporters!

KURT ZOUMA

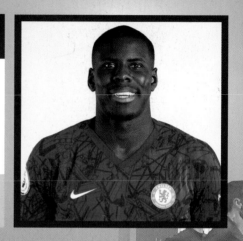

Position: Defender
Date of birth: 27.10.94
Nationality: French
Signed from: St-Etienne
CFC apps: 71   CFC goals: 4

Did You Know? Match of the Day pundit Danny Murphy has compared Kurt to Marcel Desailly, who is a former Chelsea captain and World Cup winner with France.

PLAYER PROFILES

MASON MOUNT

Position: Midfielder
Date of birth: 10.01.99
Nationality: English
Source: Chelsea Academy
CFC apps: 0

Did You Know? Mason's first taste of regular first-team football in England came under Frank Lampard at Derby County last season, when he contributed a combined 16 goals and assists for the Rams.

ROSS BARKLEY

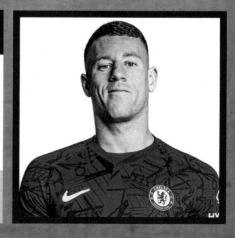

Position: Midfielder
Date of birth: 05.12.93
Nationality: English
Signed from: Everton
CFC apps: 52   CFC goals: 5

Did You Know? Ross scored his first three Premier League goals for Chelsea in consecutive matches against Southampton, Man United and Burnley during the autumn of 2018.

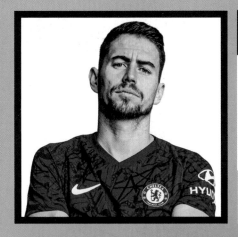

JORGINHO

Position:	Midfielder
Date of birth:	20.12.91
Nationality:	Italian
Signed from:	Napoli
CFC apps:	54

CFC goals: 2

Did You Know? No Premier League player made more passes than Jorginho in his debut season for the club, who averaged 84 passes per match for a total of 3,118.

N'GOLO KANTE

Position:	Midfielder
Date of birth:	29.03.91
Nationality:	French
Signed from:	Leicester City
CFC apps:	142

CFC goals: 8

Did You Know? Since moving to England in 2015, N'Golo has won a trophy every season, including two Premier League titles.

PLAYER PROFILES

MATEO KOVACIC

Position:	Midfielder
Date of birth:	06.05.94
Nationality:	Croatian
Signed from:	Real Madrid
CFC apps:	51

Did You Know? Mateo was a Champions League winner three times with Real Madrid before adding a Europa League triumph as a Blue last season.

RUBEN LOFTUS-CHEEK

Position:	Midfielder
Date of birth:	23.01.96
Nationality:	English
Source:	Chelsea Academy
CFC apps:	72

CFC goals: 12

Did You Know? With his Europa League hat-trick against BATE last season, Ruben became the first English player to net a Euro treble for the club since 1971!

All stats correct ahead of the 2019/20 season.

TAMMY ABRAHAM

Position: Forward
Date of birth: 02.10.97
Nationality: English
Source: Chelsea Academy
CFC apps: 2

Did You Know? After returning from a loan spell with Aston Villa, Tammy became the first Englishman to wear the No9 shirt for Chelsea since midfielder Steve Sidwell in 2008!

MICHY BATSHUAYI

Position: Forward
Date of birth: 02.10.93
Nationality: Belgian
Signed from: Marseille
CFC apps: 53   CFC goals: 19

Did You Know? Michy's goal against West Brom clinched the 2016/17 Premier League title for the Blues!

PLAYER PROFILES

OLIVIER GIROUD

Position: Forward
Date of birth: 30.09.86
Nationality: French
Signed from: Arsenal
CFC apps: 63   CFC goals: 18

Did You Know? Olivier's tally of 11 Europa League goals in the 2018/19 season made him the first Chelsea player to score 10 times in a European campaign for the club.

CALLUM HUDSON-ODOI

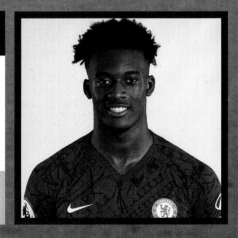

Position: Forward
Date of birth: 07.11.00
Nationality: English
Source: Chelsea Academy
CFC apps: 28   CFC goals: 5

Did You Know? Callum is England's fifth-youngest debutant in the post-war era after making his first appearance for the Three Lions at the age of 18 years and 136 days!

PEDRO

Position: Forward
Date of birth: 28.07.87
Nationality: Spanish
Signed from: Barcelona
CFC apps: 182   **CFC goals:** 41

Did You Know? Pedro is one of five players to score in the final of both major UEFA competitions, a list which also includes former Chelsea striker Hernan Crespo.

CHRISTIAN PULISIC

Position: Forward
Date of birth: 18.09.98
Nationality: American
Signed from: Borussia Dortmund
CFC apps: 0

Did You Know? When he was seven, Christian spent a year living in England and trained with the juniors of non-league side Brackley Town!

PLAYER PROFILES

WILLIAN

Position: Forward
Date of birth: 09.08.88
Nationality: Brazilian
Signed from: Anzhi Makhachkala
CFC apps: 292   **CFC goals:** 52

Did You Know? Willian was a late call-up to the Brazil squad for last summer's Copa America, but he played a key role in helping his country win the trophy for the first time since 2007.

All stats correct ahead of the 2019/20 season.

N'GOLO
KANTE

CHRISTIAN
PULISIC

ANDREAS

1 Which Italian club did Chelsea sign Antonio Rüdiger from in 2017?

a) AC Milan   b) Juventus   c) Roma

2 Who became only the second person to win the Copa America with their national team while a Chelsea player, after former centre-back Alex, in 2019?

a) Marcos Alonso   b) Willy Caballero   c) Willian

3 Which Chelsea star is the only outfield player to have won back-to-back Premier League titles with different clubs, in 2016 and 2017?

a) Ross Barkley   b) Danny Drinkwater   c) N'Golo Kanté

4 Jorginho and Emerson Palmieri were both born in Brazil, but which European country do they play their international football for?

a) Italy   b) Russia   c) Spain

5 For which club did Tammy Abraham score 26 goals in the Championship while on loan in 2018/19?

a) Aston Villa   b) Cardiff City   c) Sheffield United

QUIZ-TENSEN

6 Which Premier League side did Kurt Zouma spend the 2018/19 season on loan with?

a) Everton   b) Newcastle United   c) Watford

7 Which of these Chelsea youngsters did not play for Frank Lampard at Derby County?

a) Reece James   b) Mason Mount   c) Fikayo Tomori

8 Who started their professional career with Spanish side Barcelona?

a) Marcos Alonso   b) Kepa Arrizabalaga   c) Pedro

9 Who played every minute of Chelsea's 2018/19 Premier League campaign?

a) Cesar Azpilicueta   b) Jorginho   c) Mateo Kovacic

10 Christian Pulisic was given his international debut for the USA by which former Premier League striker turned manager?

a) Didier Drogba   b) Jurgen Klinsmann   c) Alan Shearer

AMERICAN DREAMER: CHRISTIAN PULISIC

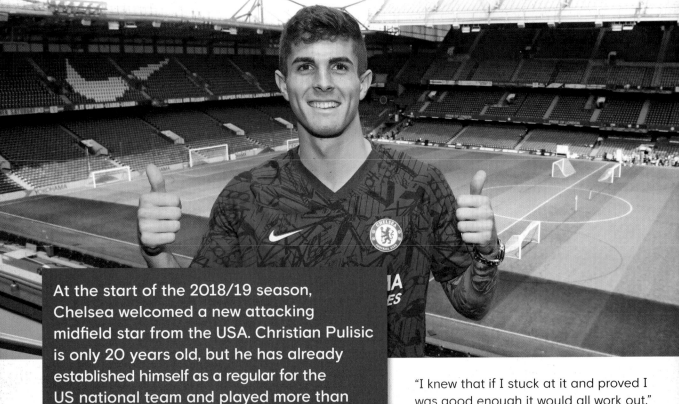

At the start of the 2018/19 season, Chelsea welcomed a new attacking midfield star from the USA. Christian Pulisic is only 20 years old, but he has already established himself as a regular for the US national team and played more than 125 games for German giants Borussia Dortmund. Here's all you need to know about our American newcomer...

"I knew that if I stuck at it and proved I was good enough it would all work out," he explained, giving great advice to youngsters who believe in their talent. "If they see you can play, they respect you."

Adventurer

Christian Pulisic was born in Hershey, Pennsylvania, in the north-east of the United States. It's the town that gives its name to one of the most famous chocolate bars in America, but he didn't stay there too long. In fact, at the age of 15, he made the decision to move across the Atlantic Ocean to continue his football education in Germany, with Borussia Dortmund. It was a tough period in his life.

"I knew that move wasn't going to be easy, and the first two years in Germany were very tough for me," he said. "A foreign country, a new language, being away from my family and friends – I thought people were looking at me, asking: 'Who is this American trying to take my spot?'"

In the end, his brave move paid off brilliantly, as two years later he was in the Dortmund first team and he won the German Cup in 2017.

Record breaker

Pulisic emerged on the scene at a very young age, and he has the records to prove it. He scored his first goal for Borussia Dortmund when he was just 17, making him the youngest non-German goalscorer in the history of the German Bundesliga. Soon afterwards, he became the youngest player of any nationality to score two goals in a Bundesliga game and he even made his Champions League debut before he turned 18. The records have poured in at international level as well, as he became the youngest player both to represent and to score for the USA in a World Cup qualifier. He certainly began his career with a bang – let's hope he keeps setting new standards in the blue of Chelsea!

English experience

When he was seven years old, Pulisic spent a year living in England and played for the youth team of Brackley Town, a local team to the Oxfordshire village where he was living. It was his first taste of life and football in this country, but now he is back with one of the biggest teams in the land. He can't wait to get started as a Blues star and has his eyes set on winning the biggest trophies in the game. As he said when he arrived at Stamford Bridge in the summer: "Chelsea ... there's a champion mentality at this club."

FORMER BLUES IN AMERICA

As Christian Pulisic looks to make waves as an American in London, we take a look at the ex-Chelsea players who headed across the Atlantic Ocean in the other direction to test themselves in the United States, beginning all the way back in the 1920s...

Harold Brittan

A lethal striker who took the United States by storm in the 1920s, Brittan played for teams called Bethlehem Steel and Fall River Marksmen during the days when the American Soccer League was as big as the best European leagues. He scored more than a goal a game for both those clubs and won four league titles in the USA. He didn't have much time at Chelsea because he had to leave to serve in the army during the First World War. In total he played 24 times and scored seven goals in three seasons at Stamford Bridge. However, he is remembered as one of the all-time greats in America, and was even inducted into the US Soccer Hall of Fame.

John Dempsey

In the summer of 1978, two Chelsea heroes made their way to Pennsylvania to join a North American Soccer League team called Philadelphia Fury. The first was the great Blues striker, Peter Osgood, whose statue stands outside the West Stand at Stamford Bridge, but it was his team-mate John Dempsey who made the bigger impact in the USA's new league, which was known as the NASL. Dempsey was a no-nonsense centre-back, who had become a Chelsea hero when he scored the winning goal against Real Madrid in the 1971 European Cup Winners' Cup final. He enjoyed three good years in Philadelphia and was named the NASL's Defender of the Year in 1979.

Charlie Cooke

Another star of the same era was Charlie Cooke, whose wing play for Chelsea made him one of the fans' favourites in his two spells at Stamford Bridge. Cooke, who was a key part of the Blues' FA Cup and European Cup Winners' Cup squads in 1970 and 1971, moved to the United States in 1976, where he starred for LA Aztecs, Memphis Rogues and California Surf, before staying on to play in an indoor league with Calgary Boomers, Cleveland Force and Dallas Sidekicks. Cooke still lives and works in the United States, running a soccer school in Cincinnati, Ohio.

John Spencer

The Scottish forward, who became a favourite of the Chelsea faithful between 1992 and 1997, made the move to America in 2001, joining MLS team Colorado Rapids. He had a debut season to remember, scoring 14 times to earn a place in the MLS Best XI. He repeated both feats two years later, when he was also among the nominees for the MLS MVP Award, which is given to the most important player in the league. Spencer retired in 2004 to take up coaching, and in 2010 he was named the first head coach of another MLS team, Portland Timbers, where he remained in charge for four seasons.

Frank Lampard

Chelsea's all-time highest scorer with 211 goals in 648 appearances, Lampard was the Blues' midfield marvel between his arrival from West Ham in 2001 and his departure in the summer of 2014. He won three Premier League titles, four FA Cups, two League Cups as well as the Champions League and the Europa League here. Later, he played two MLS seasons with New York City FC, in 2015 and 2016, excelling in his last year with 12 goals in 19 league games as his side reached the MLS Cup Playoffs for the first time.

Didier Drogba

Chelsea's 2012 Champions League final hero first headed to North America when his second spell in London came to an end in 2015. He initially moved to Canada, joining Montreal Impact, where he scored 21 goals in 33 MLS appearances over the course of two campaigns, including 11 in 11 games in the 2015 regular season as he helped the team to the MLS Cup Playoffs. Drogba then headed south to become a player-owner of Phoenix Rising, in a lower league called the USL, where he won the Western Conference at the age of 40.

Ashley Cole

Once considered by many to be the best left-back in the world, England international Cole was part of a solid Chelsea defence alongside John Terry in the late 2000s. He won every major domestic and European trophy with the Blues between 2006 and 2014 and has won the FA Cup more times than any player in history, having picked up seven winners' medals. In America, he played for LA Galaxy, making 89 MLS appearances between 2016 and 2018.

ACADEMY:
DRAMA IN EUROPE!

It wasn't just the men's team enjoying themselves in Europe last season. Chelsea's Under-19s went all the way to the UEFA Youth League final in 2019, and just missed out on the biggest trophy at that age level. It was a dramatic run for Joe Edwards' team, full of twists, turns and penalty heroics. Let's take a look back at the best bits...

A GOAL-DEN START

Chelsea have won the UEFA Youth League twice and reached the final four times in the tournament's six-year existence, making them the most successful club in its short history. This year, however, they had to take a different route to get there. As national youth champions, we entered the competition through the champions side of the draw, and that meant playing two games against other teams that had won their national youth league titles the previous season. In the end, both rounds turned into goal-fests as we beat Norwegian champions Molde 14-1 on aggregate, then defeated Sweden's finest, Elfsborg, 9-0 over two legs!

28

KNOCKOUT NAIL-BITERS

We began the knockout stage, where the games are played over one leg, with a 3-1 win over Monaco, before playing French side Montpellier in the Round of 16 – and this time it was much tougher. Playing at the Chelsea Academy in Cobham, we had to wait until the 72nd minute to take the lead through Juan Castillo, but Montpellier equalised six minutes later and then came on strong. Thankfully, captain Luke McCormick popped up with a late winner to send us through to the quarter-finals.

The next round proved to be even trickier. Dinamo Zagreb, of Croatia, went 2-0 up at Cobham and we looked in serious trouble. However, McCormick scored twice in the last 13 minutes to level the scores and take the game to a penalty shootout, which we won 4-2. Karlo Ziger made two fine saves from the spot, and defender Marc Guehi went viral on social media by scoring his penalty without even taking a run-up!

FINALS WEEKEND

The semi-finals and the final of the UEFA Youth League are played over a single weekend at the UEFA headquarters in Nyon, Switzerland. Chelsea's Under-19s were drawn to play Barcelona and it was a game that everyone wanted to see. The standard of play was incredible and the Spanish team had the lead twice, only for Chelsea to equalise on both occasions, thanks to McCormick and Charlie Brown. Once again, it went to a penalty shootout, and once again goalkeeper Ziger was the hero as Chelsea won 5-4 to make yet another final.

Sadly, the final proved to be a step too far, as we fell to a 3-1 defeat at the hands of Porto. It was a great journey, however, and Blues striker Charlie Brown (pictured) ended as the competition's highest scorer with 12 goals. In total, Chelsea bagged 33 goals altogether, which made us the highest-scoring team in the tournament. "I don't think the boys could have given any more and I'm proud of the way they played," said their coach Joe Edwards after the final.

PLAYER

History was made at the 2019 Chelsea Awards ceremony in Londo as several records were broken, with the players and staff from ou men's, women's and Academy sides gathered alongside supporter to celebrate our top performers from the 2018/19 season.

RECORD BREAKER

For the first time ever, all three of our men's senior awards were taken home by the same player, as Eden Hazard said farewell to Chelsea in style. The Belgian had already been given the Players' Player of the Year trophy by his team-mates at Cobham, but added Player of the Year before his amazing solo strike against Liverpool was revealed as Goal of the Season. That was the fourth time Hazard had been named Chelsea's Player of the Year – having also won in 2014, 2015 and 2017 – more than anyone else.

Eden Hazard with Player of the Year and Goal of the Season trophies and scoring his Goal of the Season against Liverpool

RISING

Teenage winger Callum Hudson-Odoi was named our Young Player of the Year after breaking into the senior team during last season. A dramatic campaign saw the popular youngster make 24 first-team appearances, scoring five goals and playing a big part in our run to the Europa League final. His performance for the Blues were so impressive he even made his international breakthrough as he was handed his senior debut for England at the age of 18.

Callum Hudson-Odoi with Young Player of the Year trophy

AWARDS

LEADING LADIES

Chelsea Women were also honouring their best players from 2018/19 at the awards night, but unlike the men's team the fans and players were split on their decision. The supporters picked Erin Cuthbert as Player of the Year, after the Scottish international scored in every round as we made it to the Champions League semi-finals. However, the Chelsea Women squad chose Sophie Ingle as their Players' Player of the Year, rewarding the Welsh midfielder for an excellent first season back at the club.

Sophie Ingle and Erin Cuthbert with Chelsea Women manager Emma Hayes

ONE FOR THE FUTURE

Conor Gallagher was chosen as our Academy Player of the Year after an impressive season with the development squad, as well as playing a vital role in the Chelsea Under-19s' run to the UEFA Youth League final. The local boy has been with the Blues since he was six years old and been a regular in midfield as he has risen up the age groups, including captaining our Under-18s on the way to winning the FA Youth Cup in 2018.

Conor Gallagher receiving Academy Player of the Year award from development squad head coach Joe Edwards

SERIAL WINNERS

Eden Hazard became the first four-time Chelsea Player of the Year winner, but he's far from the only player to win the award multiple times. Here are the other 10 former Blues who the fans have chosen as their star man on more than one occasion.

JOHN HOLLINS
(1970 and 1971)

In an era when Peter Osgood was scoring goals for fun and Peter Bonetti was a heroic presence in the Chelsea goal, Hollins' contribution to Chelsea's FA Cup and Cup Winners' Cup triumphs at the start of the 1970s could have easily been overlooked. Not by the Blues faithful, who chose him as POTY in consecutive seasons.

DAVID WEBB
(1969 and 1972)

Our 1970 FA Cup hero was a defender by trade, but Webby did the lot. He scored goals, including a hat-trick in one game against Ipswich, kept a clean sheet as an emergency goalkeeper against those poor old Tractor Boys but, most importantly, he was a tough-tackling, head-anything defender who played each game as if it was his last!

CHARLIE COOKE
(1968 and 1975)

Few in blue have ever been blessed with as much talent as the former Scotland international known as the Bonnie Prince, whose dazzling dribbles and precise passes made him a favourite with supporters and his attacking team-mates who were the beneficiaries of his generosity. Check out the video section on Chelsea's website to see his incredible cross for Osgood in the 1970 FA Cup final.

RAY WILKINS
(1976 and 1977)

Butch wasn't even out of his teens when he won his first Player of the Year award. He'd already taken on the captain's armband at the age of 18, leading a team primarily comprising his peers from the youth set-up, and he was not only a born-leader – boy, could he play as well, as he scored his fair share of goals and assisted even more.

PAT NEVIN
(1984 and 1987)

The second Scottish entrant on this list was just as talented as the first, with a penchant for a mazy dribble and elaborate set-up over putting the ball in the back of the net himself. Wee Pat ran rings around Division Two defences to lead us back into the big time and earn the first of his awards; three years later he proved he could be our star man at the highest level, too.

DENNIS WISE
(1998 and 2000)

In his award-winning seasons there was no shortage of world-class talent in our ranks, but the captain was the man fans voted for, as he combined the tenacity one typically associates with him and the technical qualities which once saw him score a great goal in the San Siro. We'd been led out of the dark ages of English football and our skipper was at the forefront of the revolution.

GIANFRANCO ZOLA
(1999 and 2003)

Zola almost led us to our first championship in 44 years when he first won the award, but his second POTY was even more impressive. In his final season at the club, at the age of 36, Zola described the campaign as "my miracle" as he helped us back into the Champions League; for a man who specialised in magic, that really is saying something.

FRANK LAMPARD
(2004, 2005 and 2009)

Super Frank was the first player to win the highest individual honour at Chelsea on three occasions. His back-to-back triumphs came in the first two years of the Roman Abramovich era, when he proved himself to be worthy of a place among the world-class talent emerging at the Bridge. Then, four years later, Lamps led us to FA Cup glory and further individual recognition.

JOHN TERRY
(2001 and 2006)

Before he was Chelsea's captain, leader, legend, JT had taken only 42 first-team matches to prove he was worthy of the accolade of being Player of the Year. Little could we have known then that after those promising first few steps, his No26 shirt would become iconic to a generation of supporters. His second POTY award came shortly after leading us to our second Premier League title on the bounce.

JUAN MATA
(2012 and 2013)

Mata's playmaking skills were a major factor in the Blues becoming the first side to lift the Champions League and Europa League in consecutive seasons. Indeed, it could easily be forgotten that the Spaniard supplied the corner kick from which Didier Drogba equalised in the former before repeating the trick for Branislav Ivanovic's late winner in the latter.

WHO SCORED?

1 This South American always points to the heavens to show his thanks when he scores a goal.

2 This music fan scored a hat-trick as we thrashed Wigan to win the Premier League title in 2010.

3 This striker's opening goal against Tottenham showed he wasn't such an old man after all, even if he celebrated like one!

4 This player's knee-slides were a regular sight at Stamford Bridge, before he decided to retire his celebration because he kept cutting his legs.

5 These acrobatic somersaults were mostly seen at the Bridge during our time playing with wing-backs, with this African international a key player when we won the title in 2017 and FA Cup a year later.

6 This Brazilian has a lot of regular goal celebrations, often seen sucking his thumb or kissing his wedding ring, but who could forget his dancing in Barcelona after scoring a wonder goal in our 2012 Champions League semi-final?

Answers on page 63

THANK YOU, GARY CAHILL!

SERIAL WINNER

Within a few months of arriving at Chelsea from Bolton Wanderers at the age of 26, Gary Cahill had won the Champions League and picked up an FA Cup winners' medal, and it was just a sign of things to come as he went on to win all the major European and domestic trophies on offer. In 2013, he made it back-to-back European successes when we won the Europa League final in Amsterdam, then two years later he completed a different double - the Premier League and the League Cup. He doubled down on his league titles in 2017 and made amends for missing his first FA Cup final at Chelsea when he captained us to glory at Wembley in 2018. No wonder he was asked to lift the trophy when we won the Europa League again just before he left at the end of last season!

BIG AT THE BACK

Cahill's defensive skills were one of the main reasons we captured so much silverware during his time here. He was a solid physical centre-back, who was good in the air and knew exactly where to position himself as well. He became a great organiser as he grew older and gained experience alongside John Terry, and it was no surprise when he became captain following JT's departure in 2017. Cahill was just as focused in a back three,

often playing on the left of the backline when we won the league playing 3-4-3 in 2016/17. His reliable performances at the back obviously earned him the respect of his opponents too, as he was voted into the PFA Premier League Team of the Year on no fewer than three occasions during his time at Chelsea, in 2014, 2015 and 2017.

England international centre-back Gary Cahill joined Chelsea in January 2012 and last season was his final year at Stamford Bridge. He won it all during his time here, and ended up as club captain. Let's look back at what made him such a special player for the Blues...

VITAL GOALS

Cahill scored 25 goals in his 290 Chelsea appearances, which is a pretty good return for a defender. He knew how to finish with his feet as well as his head and he scored on some pretty big occasions too. The pick of his goals was probably his volleyed effort in a 4-2 win over Tottenham at White Hart Lane in October 2012, and he was on target against Spurs again at Stamford Bridge in May 2016, when we fought back from two goals down to draw 2-2 and deny our London rivals a shot at Premier League glory. During our 13-game winning run in the middle of the 2016/17 campaign, Cahill was on the scoresheet in the 4-0 win over Manchester United that was arguably the pick of those remarkable consecutive wins. That proved to be his best season for goals, as he bagged eight from centre-back in his second Premier League title campaign.

NICE GUY

Cahill was one of the most popular players in the dressing room. He was loved by everyone at the club and always set a wonderful example to his fellow professionals. He will be sorely missed by everyone at Chelsea and we wish him all the best for his future career. Thanks for the memories, Gaz. You really did win it all!

Legendary Chelsea midfielder Frank Lampard returning to the club as head coach got us thinking about which current Blues stars might come back as a manager one day. Just for fun, we've gazed into our crystal ball and imagined what that could look like by combining pictures of some Chelsea players with managers from the past.

Cesar Azpilicueta

Pedro

Ross Barkley

Ruben Loftus-Cheek

Olivier Giroud

CHELSEA HISTORY: FA CUP WINNERS 1970

The 50th anniversary of one of Chelsea's greatest ever achievements is this season. Back in 1970, we had a wonderful team with stars such as Peter Osgood, Ron 'Chopper' Harris and Charlie Cooke at the heart of it. Yet, until 1970, we had just fallen short of winning the league or the FA Cup. That year, we had our best chance yet to win major silverware when we reached the FA Cup final against Leeds United. The rest is history...

THE OCCASION

At the time Leeds were one of the top teams in the country. They had won the league in 1969 and were runners up in 1970, and they had a huge rivalry with Chelsea, who were seen as one of the few teams that could get the better of them. It was our chance to show that the Blues – managed by the great Dave Sexton – were also capable of winning major trophies and the fans were desperate for the club to bring the FA Cup back to Stamford Bridge for the first time in history.

WEMBLEY

There were 100,000 people at the old Wembley Stadium for the final, but the pitch was in a terrible condition, meaning the ball didn't bounce much at all, and kept getting stuck in the mud! So it was hardly surprisingly that both teams scored scruffy goals in the first half – Chelsea's courtesy of skilful winger Peter Houseman, who was one of the stars of the run. Then, late in the game, Leeds looked to have nicked it when they went 2-1 up on 83 minutes and the white half of Wembley went berserk. Chelsea had other ideas, though, and a quick free-kick set up an even later equaliser, when John Hollins crossed for a sensational headed goal by striker Ian Hutchinson. It sounds crazy now, but in those days the final went to a replay if it was a draw after extra time, so when nobody scored in the extra 30 minutes, the two teams had to do it all again two-and-a-half weeks later!

It's hard to believe but the 1970 FA Cup final replay took place in midweek, at Old Trafford! The fact that everyone was at home watching the TV has made the game one of the most famous club football matches in English history. It was shown on both BBC and ITV and, incredibly, more than 28 million people tuned in, across the United Kingdom, to watch the second game between Chelsea and Leeds. That's more than half the population switching on their TV sets to see who would take home the Cup!

It was a bad-tempered match with heavy tackles flying in everywhere, and Leeds went 1-0 up at half-time. However, Chelsea fired back in the second half and equalised with 12 minutes left thanks to a magnificent diving header by Osgood. Peter Bonetti was immense in the Chelsea goal at the other end, as things got increasingly tense. The game went to extra time, but we finally made the break through when a huge long throw by Hutchinson was flicked to the back post, where David Webb headed it in to secure Chelsea' first-ever FA Cup.

The trophy success meant a great deal to the club and the supporters and the parade down the Fulham Road was an amazing sight. Chelsea fans and local well-wishers absolutely packed the streets around Stamford Bridge, to the point where people were climbing trees and telephone boxes just to get a glimpse of the FA Cup and Sexton's heroic team that had won it for them. Since then, we have gone on to win the famous old competition another seven times, but 1970 will always be the first.

DOUBLE, DOUBLE, DOUBLE!

DOUBLE WINNERS

"Double, Double, Double – John Terry has won the Double!" is a song you've heard over and over at Stamford Bridge. It harks back to an incredible season at Stamford Bridge a decade ago, when the Blues made history by winning the Premier League and FA Cup in the same season, with the goals flying in at an incredible rate.

Italian job

The man leading Chelsea towards our Double was Carlo Ancelotti, a legendary former player and manager with AC Milan. Carletto, as he is known in his homeland, had a reputation for getting the best out of big-name players and that certainly proved to be the case in west London. He was ably assisted by Ray Wilkins, a man who had Chelsea running through his veins, and together they formed a wonderful double act.

Champions!

The Premier League title race went all the way to the final day of the season and, crucially, we were masters of our own destiny with a narrow lead over Manchester United. Our opponents were Wigan Athletic and what followed was beyond most Blues fans' wildest dreams, as we smashed eight – yes, you read that correctly – past the Latics to record our biggest top-flight victory! What's more, we became the first side to pass 100 Premier League goals in a season, and the celebrations went on long into the night!

Cup Kings!

While SW6 partied to celebrate the title, the players prepared to put the icing on the cake by adding the FA Cup to the trophy cabinet. Relegated Portsmouth were our opponents at Wembley but there was no chance of a fairytale ending with Drogba in town! The Ivorian centre-forward curled home a stunning free-kick and Petr Cech saved a penalty in the second half to secure our first Double and ensure it was a season we'll never forget.

20/20

One of the keys to our success was the goalscoring form of Didier Drogba and Frank Lampard. For only the second time in Premier League history – a tally which has since moved on to four – one team had two players pass the 20-goal mark in the same season. Drogba secured the Golden Boot award given to the top scorer in the division, having netted 29, and Super Frank also provided more assists than any other player, to go along with the 22 he scored.

Golden Cole

There was plenty of goalscoring talent in our squad that season, but the pick of the bunch came not from a striker or midfielder, but a player who specialised in keeping the opposition out at the other end! Ashley Cole won our Goal of the Season award after his sensational effort in a thumping win over Sunderland, when he controlled a pin-point long pass by JT, before skipping inside a defender and finishing with aplomb.

When it counts

Plenty will point to the four victories of seven goals or more as the reason for our success that season, but actually it was the tricky matches away to our rivals which ultimately secured us the title. After a 3-0 win over Arsenal at the Emirates before the end of 2009, we then beat both Manchester United and Liverpool at Old Trafford and Anfield respectively, as well as defeating all three sides at Stamford Bridge earlier in the season. It will surprise no one that Drogba scored in the trio of away victories – has there ever been a better player for the big occasion?

Young ones

While it's a season which will mainly be remembered for the success of our men's team, let's not forget our Under-18s. FA Youth Cup triumphs have been an almost annual occurrence at Chelsea in recent years, but in 2010 we lifted the trophy for the first time in 49 years! Dermot Drummy, who sadly passed away in 2017, was our manager and captain Connor Clifford fittingly scored the winning goal in the final against Aston Villa.

SOCCER AID

Some of the biggest names in show business and sport – including several Chelsea legends – got together at Stamford Bridge in the summer as the Blues' home played host to Soccer Aid for the first time.

1 CLASH OF THE TITANS

With so many ex-Chelsea players involved, their respective battles all over the pitch were among the major pre-match talking points. Seeing Didier Drogba and John Terry go head-to-head was as epic as we expected, and for the sake of diplomacy we'll say it was honours even between the two legends!

2 ONE GAME FOR ALL

Football is a sport which prides itself on inclusivity, so it was great to see former female footballers involved in Soccer Aid for the first time. Among them was Katie Chapman, the greatest captain in the history of Chelsea Women, and there was no quarter given on either side when she came up against former Blues midfielder Michael Essien!

3 FREESTYLER

The F2 Freestylers lined up at the Bridge on opposite sides, with Jeremy Lynch representing England and Billy Wingrove on the World XI team. Between them the two skills specialists have got over 50 million followers across the various social media platforms – and they gained a few more after Lynch netted two excellent goals to give England a 2-0 advantage.

4 BOLT FROM THE BLUE

Usain Bolt is an eight-time Olympic gold medallist and he added to his collection of career highlights by scoring the goal which brought the World XI back into the contest. Brilliantly, the sprint king's shirt number was 9.58 – unconventional for a footballer, but a reminder of his world record time, in seconds, for running 100m. Unfortunately, Usain's choice in football clubs is not quite as impressive, as he is a big fan of Manchester United!

5 BALLON D'ORA

The half-time entertainment was provided by Rita Ora, but the singer might want to put her name forward for the main event next time. She showed great composure to slot home a penalty after lighting up the Bridge during the interval!

6 TOUGH TEST

Chelsea fan Joe Wicks was living out a boyhood dream by playing at Stamford Bridge, but he probably would have preferred an easier opponent to come up against than Brazilian legend Roberto Carlos!

7 GAME, CET AND MATCH

With England on the verge of recording their sixth win from eight Soccer Aid matches, former Love Island star Kem Cetinay popped up with a beautiful finish late on to send the game to a penalty shoot-out for the second year running...

8 WORLD XI SPOT ON

In 2018 it was England who emerged victorious on penalties, but this time the hero was World XI keeper Nicky Byrne of Westlife, who was once on the books at Leeds United, as the Irishman saved penalties from Wicks and Lee Mack to help his team to glory.

9 UNICEF THE REAL WINNER

It was all selfies and celebrations for the World XI after the game, but the true winner on the night was Unicef, for whom more than £6.7m was raised. The motto for Soccer Aid for Unicef is very simple: It's so much more than the world's biggest celebrity football match, it's about raising funds so that children everywhere can have the

WORDSEARCH

H	P	G	H	R	M	B	F	R	L	C
H	N	M	B	O	B	Q	F	K	M	V
O	D	O	O	E	D	D	V	C	H	Y
L	I	E	W	T	H	D	C	B	T	X
L	L	T	Q	Y	I	R	L	R	N	F
I	L	T	B	J	E	L	E	E	B	C
N	A	A	T	A	T	H	L	F	W	N
S	I	M	D	L	C	V	D	E	K	T
L	V	I	Q	O	T	T	L	L	H	T
Y	E	D	D	G	U	L	L	I	T	S
K	Z	N	O	S	T	R	E	B	O	R

Frank Lampard is the 11th person to have been both a Chelsea player and manager but can you find the names of the other 10 in this wordsearch. Good luck!

Di Matteo	McCreadie
Docherty	Robertson
Gullit	Shellito
Hoddle	Vialli
Hollins	Webb

CHELSEA

Here's your guide to everything you need to know about Emma Hayes' star-studded squad. Following a rare trophyless season, Chelsea FC Women will be looking to reclaim our spot as the top English club in the 2019/20 campaign.

TROPHY TRAIL

Chelsea Women have been the most successful side in English football over the past few years, which is incredible when you consider we only won our first silverware in 2015! That was the FA Cup, when we beat Notts County to lift the trophy in the first final held at Wembley Stadium. Since then we've added two WSL titles and another FA Cup – and all of this silverware has come in two seasons, as we've twice done the league and cup Double. Clearly, we don't do things by halves! We also won the Spring Series trophy, which was in 2017 at the end of a shortened league campaign.

WOMEN

Adelina Engman

Anita Asante

SO NEAR, YET SO FAR

The 2018/19 season may have ended without silverware, but there was barely a dull moment along the way as Emma Hayes' squad reached the semi-finals of three cup competitions, including the Champions League for the second year in a row. Ultimately, though, we came up just short – with our last-four defeat to Lyon in Europe's premier club competition hurting the most, as we outplayed the best side in the world and should have come away with the victory. It will be an all-out-assault in 2019/20 to return to our place at the top of English football and get ourselves back in European competition.

Bethany England

EMMA HAYES' BLUE AND WHITE ARMY

Our manager is Emma Hayes, who took the reins in 2012 and has helped turn the club from also-rans to one of the best in Europe! The gaffer had to end her playing career with Arsenal early because of injury, but she has more than made up for that with a managerial career which started in America and has seen her win loads of trophies for Chelsea. The fans love her as she gets her tactics spot on and always tells it like it is!

Deanna Cooper

Drew Spence

ENGLAND FOR ENGLAND

A familiar song can be heard ringing around Kingsmeadow at any Chelsea Women game: "England for England!" The chant is directed at Bethany England, who the supporters feel should be involved with the Lionesses – and they certainly make a good point, as the striker's 22 goals in 2018/19 made her the club's leading scorer! Combined with her selfless running and intelligent link-up play, is it any wonder Beth is such a favourite with supporters and team-mates alike?

Erin Cuthbert

ERIN'S EURO WORLDIE

Although our Champions League run came to an agonising conclusion with a narrow semi-final defeat to Lyon, Erin Cuthbert's goal against the eventual winners was voted as the best goal in the competition last season. It was a stunning half-volley from the edge of the box and played a part in earning her a spot in the Champions League squad of the season, alongside Karen Carney and Millie Bright. She also won Chelsea Women's Player of the Year award!

Fran Kirby

Hannah Blundell

PFA TEAM OF THE YEAR

Three Chelsea Women players were named in the 2018/19 PFA Women's Team of the Year: Hannah Blundell, Ji So-Yun and Erin Cuthbert. While it was a first selection for our young Scot, Blundell appeared for the second consecutive year and Ji was named for the fourth time, which is the joint-highest by any player in the six seasons the team has been voted for!

LIGHTS, CAMERA, ACTION!

This season a film crew will be following the girls every step of the way for a new documentary called Flying High, which will detail life at one of the world's top female football clubs. It is being produced by Fulwell73, the company behind acclaimed football documentaries Class of '92 and Sunderland 'Til I Die.

END OF AN ERA

Karen Carney announced her retirement from professional football following the World Cup, bringing to an end a career which saw her win just about every major honour in club football. The former Blues skipper spent more than three years with the club and we'll never forget her nerveless penalty which helped win us the Spring Series trophy in 2017.

JOIN US AT KINGSMEADOW

Chelsea Women play their home matches at Kingsmeadow, which is in Kingston-upon-Thames and only a few miles away from Stamford Bridge. Tickets for Barclays WSL fixtures cost £1 for kids and senior citizens and £9 for adults. You can find more information on chelseafc.com.

SOCIAL MEDIA

You can follow us across social media, where you'll get to see all the best goals, selfies, behind-the-scenes action and much more from your favourite Chelsea Women players! Find us on:

 ChelseaFCW   @ChelseaFCW   ChelseaFCW

Jess Carter

Jonna Andersson

Magdalena Eriksson

Maren Mjelde

Maria Thorisdottir

Millie Bright

Ramona Bachmann

Ji So-Yun

Sophie Ingle

WOMEN'S WORLD CUP

The 2019 Women's World Cup in France captured the imagination of the British public like never before, and a number of Blues players played a pivotal role in a tournament which could help take women's football to the next level.

Record viewing figures

A peak audience of 11.7 million tuned in to the BBC's coverage of England's heartbreaking semi-final defeat to the USA, a game which saw Carly Telford, Millie Bright and Fran Kirby represent the Lionesses as Phil Neville's side reached the last four of a major tournament for the third successive time.

Pride of London worldwide

In all, six nations benefited from the presence of a total of 11 Chelsea players throughout the month-long competition in France, with mixed results, and though none will return to Kingsmeadow with a winner's medal around their neck, their impact can be measured in other ways.

Bronze for Sweden

Our English contingent were expected to go the furthest in the tournament, but it was our two Swedes who performed best as they came home with the bronze medal! Magda Eriksson (pictured) and Jonna Andersson, along with our former keeper Hedvig Lindahl, helped the Scandinavian country overcome England after both sides lost in the semi-finals.

Dunn deal

Although none of our players were able to bring home the trophy, Blues fans were delighted to see a popular former player from our recent past help USA to glory. Crystal Dunn, an energetic left-back who made a big impact in her 18 months with the club, was a pivotal member of the team which defeated Netherlands in the final.

Home advantage

The next major international tournament is the European Championship, which takes place here in England in 2021. Can the Lionesses, after three straight semi-final appearances on the big stage, go one step further?

SP⚲T THE DIFFERENCE

Here's a chance to test your skill by spotting the 10 differences between these pictures of Cesar Azpilicueta and Ruben Loftus-Cheek celebrating a Chelsea goal.

Answers on page 63

THE MAKING OF ME

How do you become a Chelsea player? It's a question many of you will be asking over the coming years, as you look to live the dream of pulling on the famous blue shirt at Stamford Bridge. Here are some of the experiences a selection of current Blues went through in order to make it to the very top.

PEDRO ·······················

We played lots of small games when I was a kid. Some focused on possession of the ball, or dribbling two against one, shots from outside the box, using your left foot, right foot. Practising with both feet in every training session is very important when you are young, because it means in the future you will be able to use this knowledge to your advantage. I think I am good with both my feet now because I did that.

WILLIAN ···················

I had a lot of idols growing up. Marcelinho Carioca was a very famous player at the time. He's an idol of the Corinthians fans and he played in a similar position to me. Ronaldo was phenomenal. I also looked up to Romario and Ronaldinho. For me, Ronaldinho was the number one. They were the guys I admired but I could mention a lot more names because in Brazil at that time there were a lot of good players.

MARCOS ALONSO ·····

When I played with my friends, if we didn't have a ball I remember we used to play with a crushed can of Coke. We would try and make it as close as possible to a football. We would play games for hours with it. Anything would do!

ANDREAS CHRISTENSEN ··

The academy system in Denmark is a bit different to the one here. You have school during the day, and after school, at about four o'clock, you meet up to train. You do three to four days a week, but it's not as intense as it is in England. That's why a lot of people try to leave Denmark early in their career to get more opportunities to play.

OLIVIER GIROUD ·······

I started my career at my local club Grenoble and made my debut for them in 2006. It was a great feeling, especially when it's your hometown. I grew up 20 kilometres from there, with all my friends and family, so it was very special for me to play for them. I was always obsessed by goals. I scored a lot when I was younger, so from the age of six or seven I played up front, I always liked being a striker.

RUBEN LOFTUS-CHEEK ···

At the Chelsea Academy, in the early stages it was fun but you don't realise you are improving at a high rate, from the fun drills and the races going through cones and stuff like that. At a young age you are just improving so much and it is because you are enjoying it as well. Every Tuesday and Thursday we would do technical skills, dribbling with both feet and striking it into a net. You just repeat, repeat, repeat, and subconsciously it becomes second nature.

KEPA ···················

I started at the Athletic Bilbao Academy as a nine-year-old. I'd been playing for a local team in my hometown and luckily enough there were four of us who went to the Academy, because it was a 45-minute journey to Bilbao, which we did about four times a week, and it's not easy as a nine-year-old to do that. I worked my way up in the Academy, year on year I went up in the categories and I was lucky that it was a really good Academy where I learned not just about football skills, but values as well.

ROSS BARKLEY ·········

I was playing street football and my mum heard from a friend that there was a local club I could join, so she took me down. They were called Ash Celtic and when I went down for my first game I didn't have a top, so they gave me one to wear and I scored a hat-trick. After that it was every Sunday, and at first I was a centre-half because I was a big lad at a young age. I'd take the ball, go on a dribble and score a few goals.

WILLY CABALLERO ·····

As a kid, sometimes you don't know which position you are going to play, or which is best for you. The coach decided to rotate the goalkeeper every game and try different players in that position. He put me in goal, and we won. The rest of the games we had lost. So, thank God with this luck, I started to play as a goalkeeper. That was when I was seven years old. I just remember the pitch being so big, and the goal also! As a kid you want to play and touch the ball, and as a goalkeeper at that age it wasn't the best way to enjoy football.

IT'S A CHELSEA THING

2019/20 HOME AND AWAY KITS AVAILABLE ONLINE
VISIT WWW.CHELSEAMEGASTORE.COM NOW

WIN ...a signed Chelsea shirt!

We have a Chelsea shirt signed by the men's squad to give away to one lucky fan. For your chance to receive the jersey with the autographs of all your favourite Blues stars, just answer the below question correctly.

Which player scored the first goal in our 4-1 win over Arsenal in the 2019 Europa League final?

a) Ross Barkley   **b)** Olivier Giroud   **c)** Pedro

Entry is by email only. Only one entry per contestant. Please enter **CFC SHIRT** followed by either **A**, **B** or **C** in the subject line of an email. In the body of the email, please include your full name, address, postcode, email address, phone number and date of birth and send to: frontdesk@grangecommunications.co.uk by Tuesday 31 March 2020.

Last year's lucky winner, Fin from Angus.

BEHIND THE SCENES

Join us behind the scenes at Chelsea to see what the Blues players get up to off the pitch...

Azpilicueta and Mount Mason Mount is given some "encouragement" by Cesar Azpilicueta during his forfeit for losing a training game.

Giroud Not only is Olivier Giroud a world-class centre-forward, but apparently he's also a pretty good goalkeeper. At least that's what he told us.

Alonso Marcos Alonso shows off his skills for the camera in a photo shoot at our Cobham training ground.

Team Nothing passes the time in the team hotel on an away trip for Andreas Christensen, Ross Barkley, Tammy Abraham and Marcos Alonso like a friendly game of FIFA.

Kepa Goalkeepers Kepa Arrizabalaga and Willy Caballero challenge coaching staff Henrique Hilario and Petr Cech to a game of table tennis.

Pedro Pedro knows how to celebrate a goal properly, whether it's on a pitch or in table football.

Lampard Frank Lampard might have hung up his boots to become head coach, but he's still got the skills that made him a Chelsea legend as a player.

WHERE ARE STAMFORD AND BRIDGET?

Our mascots Stamford the Lion and Bridget the Lioness love celebrating with their friends and fellow fans in the stands at a Chelsea match, but get a bit shy when there are cameras around. Can you find where they're hiding in this photo?